D1479804

The Deer with the Purple Nose

by Wayne L. Brillhart

A Rusty & Purdy Backyard Bird Adventure

The Deer with the Purple Nose

www.TheBirdBooks.com

Published by Wan Lee Publishing
www.wanleepublishing.com

Authored by Wayne L. Brillhart
Photography by Wayne L. Brillhart
Copy editing by Patricia C. Brillhart, Lora Root
Photo Editing by Stephanie A. Root
Graphic Design by Karen McDiarmid
Color Consulting by Greg Dunn

Printed and bound December 2013, #89930,
Friesens of Altona, Manitoba, Canada.

10 9 8 7 6 5 4 3 2 1

Library of Congress Control Number: 2013918941
Brillhart, Wayne

Summary: Two English Setters, Rusty and Purdy, see a deer with a purple nose. They seek the help of the backyard birds to discover how the deer got the purple nose. The Photographs of ten different birds in the book assist the readers in bird recognition as they pursue the solution to the mystery.

ISBN: 978-0-9858042-0-6

1. Backyard birds—Juvenile literature.
2. Deer—Juvenile literature.
3. Bird recognition—Juvenile literature.

Dedicated to
Rev. Donald L. Kirkland

Many thanks for the lens
that started the whole series,
for all those Greek lessons
and most of all
your friendship.

A deer with a purple nose?
Now that would make me wonder!
It couldn't be a rose;
What did that nose get under?

It was a perfect day for a new mystery.

The birds were singing and my brother, Rusty, was helping me look after the yard.

I was enjoying the sunshine when . . .

"Purdy, look over there,"
Rusty barked to me.

I turned and saw
a deer visiting the yard.

It was Dottie
and her nose
looked purple!

"Dottie," I barked.
"How did your
nose get purple?"

"My nose is not purple,"
Dottie replied as she turned and went back into the woods.

"Did Dottie's nose look purple to you?" I asked Rusty.

"It sure did," he woofed.

Bobby the Blue Jay had been listening in the tree above us.
"How could Dottie have a purple nose?" he called.
"Her nose should be brown like the rest of her.
I'm going to fly into the woods to see if it really is purple."

I noticed Terry the tufted titmouse on the seed platform.

"Tell me about Dottie's purple nose," he called.

I told Terry we would try to find out.

"Purdy! Look at the birdfeeder,"
cried Spencer the Sparrow as he flew up.

We looked to see Chip the Chipmunk on the birdfeeder.
"Get out of there, Chip! That's for the birds," I barked.

"This seed is good for chipmunks too, Purdy!"
Chip squeaked as he stuffed his cheeks.

"Chip, you were here when Dottie came by.
Did you see her purple nose?" I called back.

"No, but I saw Dottie going to the side yard earlier,"
he chattered and jumped down with his pouches full.

Spencer took Chip's spot at the birdfeeder.

"Thank you, Purdy. Now I can eat.
What were you asking about Dottie?"

"I am trying to find out about her purple nose," I woofed.

Spencer saw Carol the cardinal nearby and chirped,
"Carol, do you know about Dottie's purple nose?"

Carol called back,
"Does she have a purple nose? She was fine yesterday.
My brother Carl and I have been eating these seeds
on the ground. We didn't see Dottie."

Spencer flew away and soon
Charlie the Chickadee arrived with his friend Chester.

They didn't know about Dottie's purple nose either.

"We've been busy finding insects.
We find lots of them this time of year. I just wanted a
few of my favorite sunflower seeds," replied Charlie.

Andy the American goldfinch glided to the feeder
and began to eat a sunflower seed.

"I didn't know Dottie's nose was purple,"
he chirped when I asked about Dottie.

"I'll fly to the front yard by
the thistle feeder
to look for clues."

Harry the house finch arrived as Andy was ready to leave.

"I'll help too, Purdy," he chirped
when he learned about
the deer with the purple nose.

I talked with Ruby the red bellied woodpecker when she came to the platform.

"I'll fly up into the tall trees to look for Dottie," Ruby offered.

Meanwhile,
in the front yard,
Andy enjoyed some
thistle seeds
with his friends
but didn't find
any clues.

After the snack
he reported back
to Rusty
and me.

Terry the titmouse returned with some news.

"Carol the cardinal saw Dottie and will be here soon," tweeted Terry.

When Carol arrived she chirped,
"Purdy, I saw Dottie eating in the bushes in the side yard."

Will the white breasted nuthatch arrived in time to hear her.

"Carol is right. I saw Dottie there too,"
Will added with excitement.

"Go and see."

I remembered that Chip the chipmunk
said that he saw Dottie in the side yard earlier.
"Thanks for the clue."

He was already on his way.

So I jumped down from my doghouse and followed him.

We passed by Greta the groundhog.
She told us that she had seen Dottie by a berry tree.
We had another clue.

When we got there, we saw Ruby the red bellied woodpecker
high up in the big berry tree.
She had seen Dottie earlier under this tree.
She was pecking for bugs waiting for Dottie to return.

Rusty searched the ground for clues
while I looked in the trees.

I saw a young robin in the tree that I had not met.

"Hello. What is your name?" I called.

"My name is Ricky," he chirped.

I asked him about Dottie.

"Oh yes, I saw Dottie under this tree
eating these yummy berries," Ricky replied.

This was another clue.

Then I heard a noise and turned to see
Rocky the raccoon
over farther in the tree.

Rocky
told us he could see
Dottie coming.

Dottie came out
from the woods.

"Hi, Dottie.
How did your nose
get purple?"
I asked.

"My nose is not purple!"
Dottie answered as she began to eat
some berries on the ground.

Ripe berries sometimes fall off the tree.

After Dottie left we went to where she had been eating.
We looked for more clues.

As I looked down I noticed something,
"Rusty!" I barked.
"Look! My paw is purple."

"This is a mulberry tree with lots of ripe berries. Ripe mulberries are purple."

That was the final clue.

"Dottie rubbed her nose against ripe mulberries
when she was eating; and that's how she became
'The Deer with the Purple Nose'!"
I told Rusty and the birds.

With the help
of our friends,
Rusty and I
had solved
the
mystery.

Dottie got
mulberries
on her nose!

So, if . . .

. . . you go walking

on a summer day,

keep watch for mulberry trees . . .

… or the purple
of the berries
may get on
your hands, feet,
or knees.

Purdy's Mom's Mulberry Jam

2 lbs firm ripe mulberries
6 cups granulated sugar
1 cup water
1 package powdered pectin
1/4 cup lemon juice

1. Wash and crush the mulberries.

2. Add 1 cup water and 1/4 cup lemon juice (this should measure about 4 cups).

3. Put the berry mixture into a large kettle (at least 4 times larger than the amount of fruit you have).

4. Add the pectin and stir well

5. Place over very high heat and bring to a rapid boil, stirring often.

6. Add the sugar and stir well until completely combined.

7. Bring back to a rolling boil stirring constantly.

8. Boil for exactly 4 minutes, stirring constantly. You may reduce the heat slightly if it looks like the mixture might boil over.

9. Pour into very hot canning jars leaving 1/2 inch of space at the top of the jar. Cap with hot lid and screw tight with ring.

10. Invert jars on a wooden surface with lids down for 15 minutes.

11. Turn jars right side up and shake to distribute the fruit evenly.

12. When completely cool, label and date the jars. Then store in a cool (not refrigerated) place until needed. Makes about 4 pint jars of jam.

Spread on toast for a yummy snack!

Did the deer that posed for the book know she would be a "cover girl"?

Where the Book Came From

The Mystery at the Birdfeeder, Wayne L. Brillhart's first book, was reality. The author was contemplating a title for a second book in his series on backyard birds. He was actively taking more bird photographs when a serendipitous moment arrived.

Viewing some recently developed prints (from a camera that still used film) a strange photograph appeared. It was a photograph of a deer that looked like it had a purple nose. What a great title, he thought, *The Deer with the Purple Nose!*

There were other photographs showing a bit of purple on the nose too. Later, when the book was close to going to the publisher, another photo opportunity came about. The deer with the purple nose appeared on the author's front lawn. Now, with a Canon digital camera and a new telephoto lens, he photographed while the deer posed perfectly. The experience was a reminder of when the deer stared at the author through his dining room window for the photographs in *The Mystery at the Birdfeeder.*

After the photo shoot was over the deer casually went back to the woods to finish eating.

The author believes that the sun shining on the nose is actually what gave it the purple tinge. He came up with another reason though, making his story a fun adventure. The photo editor took some artistic license, enhancing the purple a bit to help the reader visualize the story.

In his new book, readers are introduced to some new birds along with many friends from Brillhart's first book, *The Mystery at the Birdfeeder.*

Glossary

(in order of appearance)

Blue Jay

The Blue Jay enjoys seeds and nuts, especially acorns. They have also been known to eat cold oat meal left over from breakfast. They are found in the Eastern United States, the Plains States and Southeast Canada.

Sources: 3, 5.

Tufted Titmouse

The Tufted Titmouse likes seeds, suet and insects. The bigger the seed the better as the Titmouse chooses the largest seed available when at a birdfeeder. Insects eaten include caterpillars, beetles, ants, wasps, stink bugs, and treehoppers in addition to spiders and snails. Nuts, berries, acorns and beech nuts are not too big to eat. The Tufted Titmouse can be found in the Eastern United States.

Sources: 3, 4, 5.

Chipping Sparrow

The Chipping Sparrow is found in Florida and northern Mexico in the winter, in Southern California year round, and throughout the remainder of the United States and Canada the rest of the year. During migration they are found primarily in Oklahoma, the Texas panhandle, and slightly to the West. The bright rufous cap indicates a breeding adult. The chipping sparrow enjoys seeds and is mainly a ground feeder.

Sources: 1,3, 5.

Northern Cardinal

The Northern Cardinal is a seed eater. The beak has sharp edges so it can crack open the seeds. Black-oil sunflower seeds are a favorite in addition to safflower seeds, but seeds in general along with insects, fruit and grain are enjoyed by the cardinal. The cardinals prefer eating closer to the ground or on the ground. Unlike the bright red male cardinal, the female cardinal has very different markings as seen in this photograph. The Northern Cardinal is found in the Eastern and Southern United States.

Sources 2, 3, 4, 5.

Black-capped Chickadee

In the winter months seeds, berries and plant matter account for more than half of the Black-capped Chickadee diet. The other half is animal food (insects, spiders, suet, and bits of meat from frozen carcasses). During the warmer months insects, spiders, and other animal food make up about 80-90 percent of their diet. The Black-capped Chickadee can be found from the Northern United States and Canada to the Southern portion of Alaska.

Sources: 3, 4, 5.

American Goldfinch

The American Goldfinch loves thistle seed and can also be found at birdfeeders and seed socks all year around. They frequent weedy fields and floodplains where thistles and asters grow. They inhabit most of the Northern and Eastern United States and Southern Canada during the summer and move south for the winter to inhabit all of the United States except a few cold Northern states.

Sources: 3, 5.

House Finch

The House Finch is often confused with the Purple Finch which has more coloration and additional facial markings. House Finches prefer black oil sunflower seeds, Nyjer (thistle seed) and sunflower hearts; but they are also attracted to several types of fruit trees. The House Finch can be found in the Eastern and Western United States and South into Mexico; but it is not found in the middle United States from North Dakota South to the Gulf of Mexico with a few exceptions. This distribution occurred when this western bird was transplanted to the eastern U.S. It resides all year and does not fly south for the winter.

Source 5, 6.

Red-bellied Woodpecker

The Red-bellied Woodpecker feeds on insects and finds them in the cracks in the bark of trees. When it find a birdfeeder they enjoy the seeds and will push away other birds except the Blue Jay. The Red-bellied Woodpecker can be found in most areas of the United States East of the Mississippi River.

Source: 3.

White Breasted Nuthatch

The White Breasted Nuthatch eats mainly insects and similar creatures including weevil larvae, wood-boring beetle larvae, beetles, tree hoppers, scale insects, ants, caterpillars, stinkbugs, click beetles and spiders. Also in its diet are acorns, hawthorn, sunflower seeds and sometimes corn. At birdfeeders they enjoy sunflower seeds, peanuts, suet and peanut butter. The White Breasted Nuthatch likes to feed with other birds as it feels more comfortable. If there are no titmice around the nuthatch will probably stay away also sensing danger. The White Breasted Nuthatch is found year around in most of the continental United States, Mexico and parts of Western Canada.

Source: 3.

American Robin

The American Robin is found throughout North America. In the winter it is found south of Canada and in the summer north of Mexico. The American Robin enjoys fruit and is often seen hopping across a green lawn looking for worms. The robin is attracted to dogwood, honeysuckle, juniper and mulberry trees. The robin is part of the thrush family of birds. The sighting of a robin is often considered a sign that spring is on the way.

Source: 2, 3, 5, 6.

Bibliography

(Sources)

1. National Audubon Society Pocket Guide: Familiar Birds of North America – East
   Ann H. Whitman, Editor. A Borzoi Book. Published by Alfred A. Knopf, Inc. 1986.
   Eleventh Printing 2000.

2. An Audubon Handbook Eastern Birds
   John Farrand, Jr. A Chanticleer Press Edition. McGraw-Hill Book Company 1988.

3. The Cornell Lab of Ornithology website All About Birds.
   http://www.allaboutbirds.org

4. Bird Source. Birding with a Purpose web site. www.birdsource.org.
   http://www.birdsource.org/gbbc/learning/bird-feeding-tips/what-kind-of-bird-food-should-i-use

5. A Field Guide to the Birds of Eastern and Central North America. 5th Edition.
   Roger Tory Peterson and Virginia Marie Peterson. Houghton Mifflin. 1980, 2002.

6. National Bird-Feeding Society website:
   http://www.birdfeeding.org/nbfm/most-wanted-americas-top-ten-backyard-birds/attracting-americas-top-ten-backyard-birds/house-finch.html

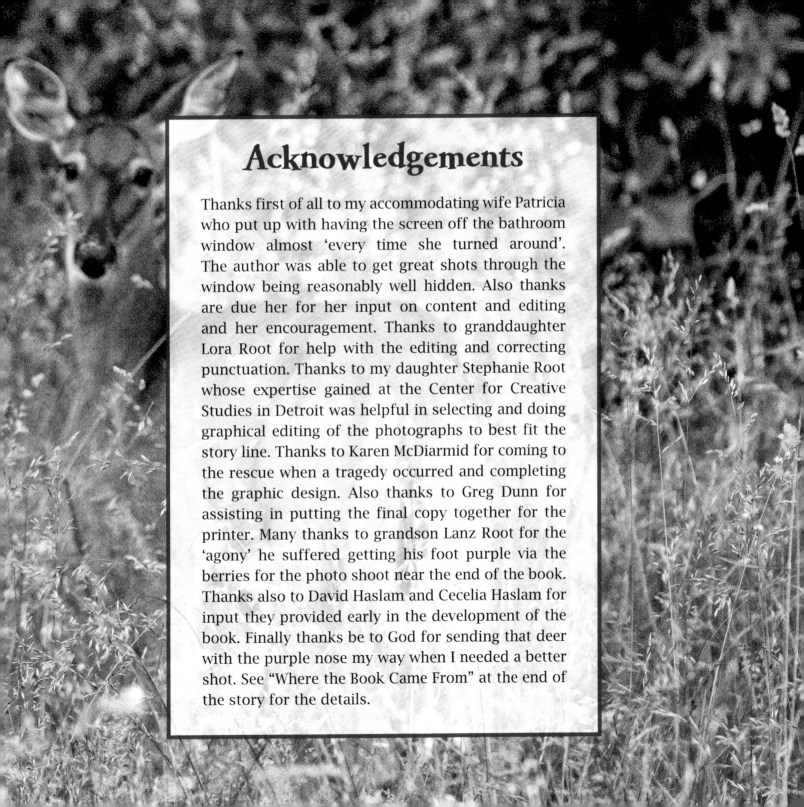

Acknowledgements

Thanks first of all to my accommodating wife Patricia who put up with having the screen off the bathroom window almost 'every time she turned around'. The author was able to get great shots through the window being reasonably well hidden. Also thanks are due her for her input on content and editing and her encouragement. Thanks to granddaughter Lora Root for help with the editing and correcting punctuation. Thanks to my daughter Stephanie Root whose expertise gained at the Center for Creative Studies in Detroit was helpful in selecting and doing graphical editing of the photographs to best fit the story line. Thanks to Karen McDiarmid for coming to the rescue when a tragedy occurred and completing the graphic design. Also thanks to Greg Dunn for assisting in putting the final copy together for the printer. Many thanks to grandson Lanz Root for the 'agony' he suffered getting his foot purple via the berries for the photo shoot near the end of the book. Thanks also to David Haslam and Cecelia Haslam for input they provided early in the development of the book. Finally thanks be to God for sending that deer with the purple nose my way when I needed a better shot. See "Where the Book Came From" at the end of the story for the details.

A Rusty & Purdy Backyard Bird Adventure
by Wayne L. Brillhart

The Mystery at the Birdfeeder

The Deer with the Purple Nose

CAMIL

Curiosity ⇨ Attention ⇨ Motivation ⇨ Involvement ⇨ Learning

The CAMIL methodology focuses on Learning. How does someone learn? It usually happens when a person is Involved in an activity or a task. The person becomes Involved as a result of Motivation. Motivation occurs after someone has focused their Attention on something. So the whole Learning process depends first on gaining Attention.

The CAMIL approach to Learning is all about using Curiosity to get Attention, then Motivation, then Involvement so that Learning takes place. In focusing on backyard birds as a subject it is hoped that the reader will recognize one (or more) of the birds when outdoors; be motivated to read more; look for more birds; and gain an excitement for Learning. A positive attitude toward learning will benefit a person for his/her entire life.